The Atheists Bible

by Garry Vaux

Published in Great Britain by
GJB Publishing

ISBN: 978-0-9576242-2-1

@Garry_Vaux
@GJBpublishing
www.GJBpublishing.co.uk

PUBLISHING

www.ingramcontent.com/pod-product-compliance
Lightning Source LLC
Chambersburg PA
CBHW071818020426
42331CB00007B/1527
* 9 7 8 0 9 5 7 6 2 4 2 2 1 *